REDEMPTION'S SECRET

Understanding the Mystery of Nisan 17, the Most Important Date in History

SHARON AUBREY

SUTTON, ALASKA

All biblical references are taken from the Authorized King James Version Bible, public domain. The use of quotes from various authors does not necessarily represent an endorsement of their theology; rather, it represents recognition of their conclusion drawn from the Scriptures or a historical source.

Cover Art: © 2018 Sharon Aubrey

© 2018 Sharon Aubrey
P.O. Box 505
Sutton, AK 99674

All rights reserved. Except as permitted under the U.S. Copyright Act of 1976, no part of this publication may be reproduced, distributed, or transmitted in any form or by any means, or stored in a database or retrieval system, without the prior written permission of the publisher.

Relevant Publishers LLC
P.O. Box 505
Sutton, AK 99674

Visit our website at www.relevantpublishers.com

Printed in the United States of America

Aubrey, Sharon
Redemption's Secret: Understanding the Mystery of Nisan 17, The Most Important Date in History/ Sharon Aubrey – 1st ed.

ISBN: 978-0-9909984-2-6
LCCN: 2018931093

DEDICATION

To Michael and Stella,

Thank you for always supporting my journeys exploring God's word.

Table of Contents

	Page
Chapter 1: Redeeming Life	1
Chapter 2: God's Calendar	7
Calculating a Day	
The Jewish Week	
Determining a Month	
Establishing a Calendar Year	
Chapter 3: The Meaning of Seventeen	16
The Hebrew Pictograph	
Seventeen in the Bible	
Chapter 4: Noah and The Ark	32
Chapter 5: Moses and The Red Sea Crossing	35
Chapter 6: Joshua and The First Fruits	45
Chapter 7: Hezekiah and The Temple	51
Chapter 8: Esther and Deliverance from Death	54
Chapter 9: The Resurrection of Jesus	
Chapter 10: Atonement: God's Design	62
Bibliography	79
Index of Illustrations and Charts	80

Chapter 1
Redeeming Life

God is the author of all life. He is the very essence of life itself. From His eternal substance, God gave life to creation, taking special care with the formation of mankind. God did not initially create Adam and Eve immortal. Instead, God planted the Tree of Life in the middle of the Garden of Eden offering Adam and Eve the choice of eternal life and encouraged them to eat from it. He also gave mankind the freedom to decide their future. This intellectual freedom has been termed "free will." Obviously, it was God's intent for mankind to eat from the Tree of Life and live forever in their perfect state of creation.

"And the Lord God commanded the man, saying,
Of every tree of the garden thou may freely eat"
Genesis 2:16

However, sadly, Adam and Eve did not choose to eat from the Tree of Life. Instead, they ate from the Tree of the Knowledge of Good and Evil, which had an eternal proclamation of death associated with it. Many people accuse God of being harsh by evicting Adam and Eve from the Garden of Eden after this event. Yet, it was mercy that motivated God to move quickly to protect His children from irreparable harm. He did not want them to compound their first mistake by consuming the fruit from the Tree of Life in a depraved state. While partaking from the Tree of Life previously would have brought the blessing of eternal life to mankind, eating from it after their fall into sin would have resulted in perpetual separation from God, with no chance of redemption.

> "So He drove out the man; and He placed at the east of the Garden of Eden cherubims, and a flaming sword which turned every way, to keep the way of the tree of life."
> Exodus 3:24

Although an eternal proclamation of death was spoken over anyone who ate from the Tree of the Knowledge of Good and Evil, God's love wouldn't allow Him to leave humanity isolated from Him in sin and death. Unfortunately, God's holiness couldn't allow Him to embrace sin or injustice either. His Word demanded the penalty of death for man's transgression. The only solution to reconcile God's love with His justice was for Him to redeem back His children by laying down His own life. Only by the exchange of God's sinless life for the guilty lives of mankind could the penalty for sin be fully paid. Death was required.

In order for a sinless God to exchange His life for humanity, He would on some level have to assume the physical form under which Adam and Eve originally received the judgment of death. Thus, God became flesh and dwelt among men on the Earth in the form known as "His son."

Chapter 1: Redeeming Life

The reality of God's incarnation is revealed by His names. Yahweh was God's covenant name with Moses and interpreted essentially meant, "I AM." Yahweh's name denoted His eternal existence as God. This was the personal name all of Israel knew to call the One, True God. Yahweh prophetically announced His future coming in the flesh through his prophets. God informed the prophets of the names He would have while in the flesh. The first name given by God for "His son" was the term "Immanuel." The name Immanuel is a Hebrew word that literally means, "God with us."

> "Therefore the Lord himself shall give you a sign; Behold a virgin shall conceive, and bear a son, and shall call his name **Immanuel**"
> Isaiah 7:14

There can be no doubt that the designation of the son being born is Immanuel. The name clearly indicates this child is more than traditional human flesh. This child is Yahweh, "God with us" in the flesh. If there was any doubt about God's intent for His son's divinity, God provided further clarification.

> "For unto us a child is born, unto us a son is given: and the government shall be upon his shoulder: and His name shall be called **Wonderful, Counselor, the Mighty God, The everlasting Father, The Prince of Peace.**"
> Isaiah 9:6

Two of the names listed above, **"Mighty God"** and **"Everlasting Father,"** can only be ascribed to Yahweh. Only God has the characteristic of existing without beginning or end: everlasting. God was never created and will never stop being. The word translated above as "everlasting" literally means "eternally existence without end." Thus, the "son" in Isaiah 9:6 is everlasting: without beginning, without end.

The name "Mighty God" leaves no doubt as to whom this son being born is. The son is the Mighty God. The phrase "Mighty God" is used repeatedly throughout the Psalms to define Yahweh. Sometimes the phrase "Mighty God of Jacob" is used to refer to Yahweh as well. Therefore, the wording in Isaiah 9:6 clearly confirms the child being born, the son being given by Yahweh is Yahweh. The Mighty God Himself will appear in human flesh to save the world.

In the Book of Zechariah, Yahweh speaks to Zechariah and proclaims He will come and live in Israel. Then ironically, the passage declares, "I will dwell in the midst of you, and you shall know Yahweh has sent me." On the surface, there appears to be a contradiction: there seems to be two individuals coming. The first is Yahweh who announced He was coming. The second is "One" coming who will be sent by Yahweh.

> "Sing and rejoice, O daughter of Zion: **for, lo, I come, and I will dwell in the midst of thee, saith Yahweh.** And many nations shall be joined to Yahweh in that day and shall be my people: **and I will dwell in the midst of thee, and thou shalt know that Yahweh of hosts hath sent me unto thee**... And He *(Yahweh)*

showed me Yehoshua, the High Priest, standing before the angel of Yahweh, and Satan was standing at his right hand to resist him."
Zechariah 2:10-3:1

To understand the complexity of what is being stated without contradiction, the next verse in Chapter 3 explains how this situation of Yahweh sending, yet simultaneously coming will progress. Zechariah sees Yehoshua (Jesus), the High Priest, standing before the angel of Yahweh. The Book of Hebrews explains that Jesus (Yehoshua) is our High Priest in Heaven, who exists eternally to make intercession for the saints. It was in His son, Yehoshua (Jesus) the High Priest for mankind, Yahweh came and was manifest to the world. Yehoshua (Jesus) was previously noted by Isaiah to be The Mighty God and The Everlasting Father. Therefore in Zechariah, we see Yahweh declaring He is the one coming, and in Yehoshua, He is also the One who was sent.

Furthermore, in the New Testament, God directed His angel, Gabriel, to inform Mary and Joseph of the name of Mary's child. His name was to be Yehoshua.

"And she shall bring forth a son, and thou shalt call his name Yehoshua (Jesus), for he shall save His people from their sins."
Matthew 1:21

The name Yehoshua (also spelled Yeshua and Yahoshua) literally means, "Yahweh saves." Through the meaning of the name, we realize who is doing the saving of the world. It is Yahweh who saves. Yahweh declared everyone who called on His name would be saved (Joel

2:32, Acts 2:21). There is no difference between calling on "Yahweh," or declaring "Yahweh Saves" by using His name/verb combination of Yehoshua (Jesus). Both names profess the same concept: Yahweh is your savior. Thus, God has fulfilled His word in Isaiah 43:10,

"I am Yahweh, and beside me there is no savior".

God's loving pursuit of mankind is the basis of the entire Bible. Within the pages of the Old Testament is a pattern of redemption occurring repeatedly on the same date in human history, Nisan 17th. The mystery revealed in analogies, spanning hundreds of years, highlighted significant turning points for both humanity and the Jewish nation. All of these important events hint towards God's pivotal redemption of mankind in Christ Jesus, which culminated in the New Testament. Aside from the birth of Adam and Eve, Nisan 17th is the most important date in human history.

Chapter 2
God's Calendar

In order to correctly understand events in the Bible, it is imperative to calculate time the way God ordained it. The Gregorian calendar used today is based on the solar calendar and does not calculate time the way God intended. As a result, many misunderstandings and misinterpretations about biblical events have been derived from errors in understanding God's timeline.

In addition to the sun and moon providing physical light to the Earth, God stated He created the sun, moon, and stars to provide humanity a way to measure time, determine appointed seasons, and to discern prophecies from Him.

> "And God said, Let there be lights in the firmament of the heaven to divide the day from the night; and let them be for signs, and for seasons, and for days, and years: And let them be for lights in the firmament of the heaven to give light upon the earth: and it was so."
> Genesis 1:14-15

Since God created the heavenly bodies to serve as a calendar for mankind, let's begin by understanding how

God ordered time. This is the first step to accurately discerning the timing of events in Scripture. The calendar used by the Jewish nation was originally based on God's timeline given in the Old Testament.

Calculating A Day

Throughout the first chapter of Genesis, God decreed a "day" as a twenty-four (24) hour period of time by recognizing first the evening, then the morning. Each period of evening (darkness) or morning (light) corresponded to approximately twelve hours.

> "And God called the light Day, and the darkness he called Night. **And the evening and the morning were the first day.**" Genesis 1:5

> "And God called the firmament Heaven. **And the evening and the morning were the second day.**" Genesis 1:8

> **"And the evening and the morning were the third day."** Genesis 1:13

> **"And the evening and the morning were the fourth day."** Genesis 1:19

> **"And the evening and the morning were the fifth day."** Genesis 1:23

Chapter 2: God's Calendar

"And God saw every thing that he had made, and, behold, it was very good. **And the evening and the morning were the sixth day.**" Genesis 1:31

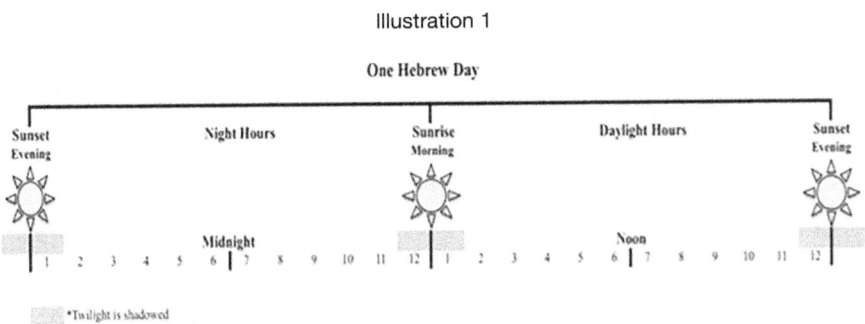

Illustration 1

Thus, the God's system for calculating a "day" begins in the evening (with sunset) and continues until the following sunset, which starts the next day.

The Jewish Week

The Hebrew calendar arranges the days of the week as God originally called them into existence in the Book of Genesis. It does not add additional words to name each day, but assigns them by the order they occur: first day, second day, third day, etc. The Hebrew word "Yom" means "day." The only day of the week to have a special name is the seventh day, which is called in Hebrew, *"Shabbat."* Shabbat is often translated into English as "Sabbath." Shabbat literally means "rest." On the first Sabbath, God rested from His work. In the Book of Exodus, God sanctifies this day as a holy day of rest for His people (Exodus 20:8-10).

Chart 1

Hebrew Word	English Translation & Equivalent
Yom Rishon	First Day (Sunday)
Yom Sheini	Second Day (Monday)
Yom Shlishi	Third Day (Tuesday)
Yom R'vi'i	Fourth Day (Wednesday)
Yom Chamishi	Fifth Day (Thursday)
Yom Shishi	Sixth Day (Friday)
Yom Shabbat	Sabbath Day (Saturday)

Below is a table depicting how the Jewish days of the week correspond to our current Gregorian calendar. As you will notice, because the day begins in the evening, each Hebrew day overlaps two days on our modern calendar.

Chart 2

Gregorian Days	Sat	Sun	Mon	Tues	Weds	Thurs	Fri	Sat
Jewish Days								
Morning	7th	1st	2nd	3rd	4th	5th	6th	Shabbat 7th
Evening	1st	2nd	3rd	4th	5th	6th	Shabbat 7th	1st

Determining a Month

Scripture also provides the calculation for measuring a month based on a lunar cycle as indicated in the Book of Psalms, chapter 104:19. The first day of the month in the original Jewish calendar began when the first sliver of the "Hodesh" (also spelled Chodesh) moon became visible after the new moon or dark of the moon. The crescent New Moon was called "Hodesh" in Hebrew which means, "to make new or renew," because it was the first time the moon was seen after being concealed in darkness at the end of the lunar cycle.

The Jewish Sanhedrin was a group of seventy elders from all the tribes originally chosen in the Book of Numbers, chapter 11, to share responsibility with Moses for leading the nation of Israel. They were responsible for determining the beginning of each new month and year. Lookouts would report to the Sanhedrin when the first sliver of the crescent moon became visible in Jerusalem. After two confirmed witnesses reported seeing the new moon, the priests would blow the trumpets indicating the first day of the month had begun. Some Scriptures supporting this pattern are Numbers 10:10 and Psalm 81:3.

During the ancient world, new months were always determined by observation. Various lookouts were appointed by the Sanhedrin to watch for the first sighting of the new moon. On cloudy nights or nights when bad weather obscured the moon, the identification of the new moon could be delayed for several days. The current Jewish calendar does not use the original biblical method of sighting the moon to determine the beginning of a new month. Instead it is based on mathematical calculations determined by Hillel II during the Fourth Century and has Pharisaical practices added to avoid concurrent Sabbaths.

Establishing A Calendar Year

The Hebrew word "Tishri" means "beginning" and is the first month of the Jewish Civil Calendar. The Civil Calendar has been used to calculate time since creation, beginning on Adam's birthday, which is identified as the first Tishri 1. As of the Gregorian year 2018 A.D., the Jewish calendar was stated to have a total of 5,778 years. The month of Tishri traditionally corresponds to the Gregorian calendar month of either September or October depending on the lunar cycle.

In the Book of Genesis and the first eleven chapters of the Book of Exodus, the Bible calculated time based on the Jewish Civil Calendar, counting from Adam's birthday. However, in the Book of Exodus chapter 12, God reset the timing of the calendar. God ordered Israel to begin calculating time with the first month of the year being Abib (traditionally spelled Aviv) instead of Tishri. Abib's name was later altered to "Nisan" after the Babylonian captivity influenced the Hebrew language. Nisan is tied to the season of Spring and corresponds to the months of either March or April depending on the annual lunar cycle.

The rearrangement of mankind's calendar by God prophetically heralded a new beginning for the world. A beginning that would not be based on Adam's birth and his sinful fall, but on the redemptive work of God through Christ Jesus, who was born to die in the month of Nisan.

Chapter 2: God's Calendar

"This month [Aviv] *shall be* unto you the beginning of months: it *shall be* the first month of the year to you." Exodus 12:2

The restructuring of the calendar by God in Exodus prompted the Jewish nation to count two calendars simultaneously. The calendar beginning with the first month of Nisan is referred to as the Religious Calendar. The other calendar, starting with Tishri, is the original Civil Calendar.

There are three months in the Old Testament, which had their names altered from the original name listed in the Bible. As a result these months have a different name associated with them in Scripture or on today's current Jewish calendar. Name alterations were a result of the Hebrews adopting Babylonian equivalent terminology during their captivity. The name changes can be confusing to people who see a different name for a month in the first few books of the Bible, and later read a different name elsewhere.

The month **"Abib"** mentioned in Exodus 13:4, 23:15; 34:18 and Deuteronomy 16:1 later became **"Nisan"** in Nehemiah 2:1 and Esther 3:7 after the influence of the Babylonian culture on the Hebrew language. Nisan is the month in which Passover always occurs. It is always tied to the annual season of spring. The month **"Zif"** mentioned in 1 Kings 6:1 and 6:37 became the month **"Iyar"** after captivity. Finally, the month **"Tishri"** was called **"Ethanim"** in 1 Kings 8:2, although not necessarily from captivity influence. While Tishri was called Ethanim once in 1 Kings, it has continued to retain the name Tishri on the Jewish calendar.

For your reference a table comparing the order of months in the Civil Calendar verses the Religious Calendar has been provided. This chart will be helpful in determining the month in which events happened in the Old Testament. The Book of Exodus chapter 12 is a turning point in biblical calculation of time. When reading any account of time prior to Exodus 12 (anything written in the Book of Genesis or the first eleven chapters in Exodus), the order of months would be calculated on the Jewish Civil Calendar. Thus, Genesis 7:11 reads as follows:

> "In the six hundredth year of Noah's life, **in the second month**, the seventeenth day of the month, the same day were all the fountains of the great deep broken up, and the windows of heaven were opened."
> Genesis 7:11

The timing of Noah's flood began in the second month. Since Tishri is the first month of the Civil Calendar, in the Book of Genesis the second month would refer to Heshvan. However, after Exodus chapter 12, time was reorganized by God and calculated according to the Jewish Religious Calendar, with Nisan beginning that calendar year. As such in the Book of Exodus chapter 40, when it states an event happened in the first month, it is referring to Nisan.

> "On the first day of the first month shalt thou set up the tabernacle of the tent of the congregation."
> Exodus 40:2

Chapter 2: God's Calendar

Jewish Order of Months

Chart 3

Order of Months	Civil Calendar	Religious Calendar
1st	Tishri	Nisan/Aviv
2nd	Heshvan	Iyar
3rd	Kislev	Sivan
4th	Tevet	Tammuz
5th	Shevat	Av
6th	Elul	Elul
7th	Abib/ Nisan	Tishri
8th	Iyar	Heshvan
9th	Sivan	Kislev
10th	Tammuz	Tevet
11th	Av	Shevat
12th	Adar	Adar

Chapter 3
The Meaning of Seventeen

The Hebrew Pictograph

To understand Nisan 17 better, one must know the meaning of the number seventeen in the Hebrew language. To understand the depth of its meaning, one must realize the Hebrew language is unlike other languages. Each letter of the Hebrew alphabet has a sound associated with it as in English. However, each letter also has a pictograph image, number, and sometimes even a word, phrase, or concept associated as well. The number seventeen is created by combining the letters "Yod," representing the number ten, and "Zayin," indicating the number seven. Thus together, Yod-Zayin, equal seventeen.

Yod (also spelled Yodh, Yud)

Yod, the smallest of all the Hebrew letters, is the most frequently occurring letter in Scripture. Being the smallest letter, Yod denotes a picture of humility. In fact, when Jacob wrestled with the Angel of the Lord in Genesis

32:24-29 and would not let go until He blessed him, the angel pronounced a change in Jacob's name. Jacob would no longer be called Jacob, but would now be called Israel. The only letter that remained of Jacob's old name was the letter Yod. Although very small, Yod was mentioned by Jesus as the "jot" in Matthew 5:18,

"Till Heaven and earth pass, one jot or tittle shall in no way pass from the law, till all be fulfilled,"

This indicated yod's significant importance to the Mosaic Law and the Word of God.

This humble, little letter is the foundation for the entire Jewish alphabet, proving God delights in using the small and weak things to confound the wise. Yod also demonstrates God's glory and power in the smallest details. Likutey Maharan noted, "The first dot with which the scribes first start writing a letter, or the last dot that gives a letter its final form is a yod." Thus, every single letter in the Jewish alphabet is formed with a Yod, which is symbolically representative of God's omnipresence in His word.

The fact Yod begins or ends every Hebrew letter and number is also reminiscent of Christ's statement that He is "the Alpha and Omega, the beginning and the end," Revelation 1:8. Since Jesus was a Jew speaking to the Apostle John, a fellow Hebrew, He would have spoken in John's natural language of Aramaic (a Jewish/Hebrew dialect). Jesus' words in Revelations 1:8 translated from Greek to Hebrew would read, "I am the Alef and the Tav." The Alef and Tav are the first and last letters of the Hebrew alphabet, basically the equivalent of "A" and "Z" in the English language.

Because Jesus is the Word of God (John 1:1), He is the Yod that begins and ends all the letters, making up the words of God. The letter Yod is also the first letter of God's name, "Yahweh," given to Moses. It is also the first letter in the spelling of Messiah's name, "Yahoshua" or "Yeshua" often translated Jesus. Yod is the first letter in the name of Israel (Yisrael) and for Jews, "Yehedim." The fact Yod begins the name of God, Jesus' name, and the name of God's chosen people is not an accident.

The pictograph associated with the letter Yod is one of "an arm" and "closed hand." Its form suggests a hand reaching toward Heaven and is associated with the meaning of "work," "power," and "worship," as the raised arm is often symbolic of praising God. Yad, the Hebraic word for "hand" demonstrates the original intent for the letter Yod, which begins the word "hand." Remarkably, the Yod letter is formed in the shape of a tallit, a Hebrew prayer shawl. The letter formation is reminiscent of a tallit worn over the head of a man, also indicative of the Yod pictograph associated with prayer and praise for this letter.

The Hebraic alphabet is also the Jewish system for calculating numerals. The first ten counting numbers (1-10) are equivalent to the first ten letters. For example: Alef the first letter in the alphabet is also the number one. Bet the second letter of the alphabet is equal to the number two. The tenth letter of the Hebrew alphabet is Yod. Therefore, Yod represents the number ten.

Ten is a distinctive number in the Bible often symbolic of God's authority, man's responsibility, and completion. Many Jewish scholars view ten as the number of "divine perfection." Below is a list of the uses of ten in the bible:

Chapter 3: The Meaning of Seventeen

- The phrase **"God said"** is used ten times in Genesis chapter 1.
- There were ten generations from Adam to Noah.
- Ten generations from the fall of man to the first mention of man finding grace in God's eyes. (Genesis 6:8).
- In the tenth month, the tops of the mountains were finally seen after the flood. (Genesis 8:5).
- For the sake of ten righteous men, God would have not destroyed Sodom and Gomorrah. (Genesis 18:32)
- Abraham gave a tenth of all his possessions to Melchizedek, King of Salem. (Genesis 14:20; Hebrews 7:2-4)
- Jacob promised God a tenth of all his possessions. (Genesis 28:22)
- God brought ten plagues upon Egypt. (Exodus 11:1-12:34)
- There were Ten Commandments given to Moses/ Israel.
- The Passover Lamb was selected on the tenth day of Nisan. (Exodus 12:3)
- The tabernacle in the wilderness was made of ten curtains of fine linen (Exodus 26:1).
- In the Holy Temple were 10 lavers, 10 lampstands, and 10 tables. (2 Chronicles 4:6-8)
- Day of Atonement is on the tenth day of Tishri. (Leviticus 23:27; 25:9)
- God demanded a tithe (a tenth part) of all that Israel owned. (Leviticus 27:32)

19

- God gave King Hezekiah the sign of turning the shadow on the sundial backward 10 degrees. (2 Kings 20:9-11)
- Ten days were given as the testing period for Daniel, Hananiah, Mishael and Azariah to prove they could stay healthy and strong by not eating food sacrificed to idols. (Daniel 1:14-15)
- On the tenth day of Nisan, Jesus entered Jerusalem on the back of a donkey with shouts of Hosanna, traditionally known as "Palm Sunday." (Matthew 21)
- Jesus spoke 10 *"I Am"* phrases in the Book of John.
- 10 lepers were healed by Jesus. (Luke 17:11-19)
- Jesus used the number 10 in many parables: 10 virgins (Matthew 25:1-13), 10 talents (Matt 25:14-30), 10 servants and 10 minas (Luke 19:12-27)
- There were 10 days between Jesus' ascension and the outpouring of the Holy Spirit on Pentecost.

Zayin

There are only eight letters in the Hebrew alphabet given special adornment by attaching three tagin or "crownlets" to them. Zayin is one of those letters, created by the Hebrew letter "Vav" having a crown on top. Thus, Zayin is considered a crowned Vav. Vav is often associated with mankind since it represents the number six, and Adam was created on the sixth day. Thus, Zayin is symbolic of the "crowned man," the completed or perfected man: Christ Jesus, the King of kings. Vav's pictograph is of a hook or

Chapter 3: The Meaning of Seventeen

nail and first is used in Genesis 1:1 to join the words and concept of "Heaven" and "Earth." Later Vav is used in constructing the Tabernacle, or dwelling place of God. It held the large curtains on the wooden posts that contained Yahweh's presence on earth. This imagery was prophetically symbolic of God being wrapped in the material or flesh in Jesus the Christ. Therefore, Zayin, the crowned Vav, is an image of Jesus, the crowned man who connects Heaven with Earth.

The letter Zayin, while having a complexity of the crowned Vav, also has its own independent pictographic associated with it. The image includes a "plowshare," "weapon," "sword," but can also represent "food" and "to nourish." All of these descriptions are indirect references to Jesus, with the sword being the most obvious inference.

Jesus said in Mathew 10:34 that He came not to send peace on earth but to send "a sword." Jesus is also described as the Word of God made flesh in John 1:1-14. Later in Ephesians 6:17, the Sword of the Spirit is revealed to be the very same Word of God. Thus, Jesus is directly associated with the image of a sword. He is the sword of God: quick and powerful sent into the world to divide the soul and spirit, discerning the hearts of men. In the Revelation of Jesus Christ to Saint John, Jesus is mentioned as having this sword of the Spirit proceed from His mouth in chapters 1:16, 2:12, 2:16, 19:15 and 19:21. There is no separation between Jesus and the sword of the Spirit. Christ is also the judge who will cause the nations to beat their swords into plowshares (Isaiah 2:4, Joel 3:10, Micah 4:3) again associating the plowshare and sword imagery of Zayin with Jesus.

While the primary meaning of Zayin is "sword," it is derived from a root word that means "sustenance" or "nourishment." Thus, the translation "to feed" can be associated with Zayin. The root "zan" (made from zayin) is in the Hebrew word "mazon," translated "food." Therefore, there appears to be a strong connection between the image of a sword, associated with war or fighting, and the concept of food.

Interestingly, the Jewish word for war, "milchamah" contains the word "lechem," which means bread. The image of "bread" inside the word "war" again ties the Zayin imagery of a sword to the root word meaning nourishment. Thus, it is no coincidence that the same Jesus, who was the sword of the Spirit, continually referred to Himself as the "lechem" or bread of life (John 6:33-51) for mankind.

In Jewish tradition, Zayin as the number seven has always been symbolic of "completion," "wholeness," "blessing," "perfection," and "rest." Seven was the first mention of Yahweh (God) resting. The following is a short list of the number seven used in Scripture.

- Genesis 1:1 is comprised of 7 Hebrew words
- God sanctified the 7th day because He rested from His work. (Genesis 2:2-3)
- Enoch, the 7th generation from Adam was translated.
- Noah was in the Ark 7 days before the Flood started. (Genesis 7:4, 10)
- God commanded Noah to take 7 pairs of clean animals and birds. (Genesis 7:2-3)
- Jacob served 7 years for Rachel.

- Blood was sprinkled 7 times on the Mercy Seat. (Leviticus 16:14)
- Blood of the sin offering sprinkled before the veil 7 times. (Leviticus 9:17)
- There were 7 days to atone for the altar to purify it. (Exodus 29:37 and Ezekiel 43:26)
- There are 7 weeks from Passover to Pentecost.
- The year of Jubilee was counted 7 x 7. (Leviticus 25:8-9)
- It took 7 years to build the Temple. (1 Kings 6:37-38)
- The Shunammite's son sneezed 7 times after Elisha raised him from the dead. (2 Kings 4:32-36)
- Naaman washed in the Jordan River 7 times to be healed of leprosy. (2 Kings 5:9-14)
- There are 7 Spirits of God, with the last being the Reverence or Fear of God. (Isaiah 11:2)
- Jesus said forgive 70 x 7 (Matthew 18:21; Luke 17:4)
- Jesus said 7 things while dying on the cross.
- Jesus healed 7 times on the Sabbath.
- The Revelation of Jesus Christ to Saint John contained:
    - 7 churches
    - 7 spirits
    - 7 golden candlesticks
    - 7 stars
    - 7 lamps

- 7 seals
- 7 horns
- 7 eyes
- 7 angels
- 7 trumpets
- 7 thunders
- 7 plagues
- 7 vials
- 7 mountains
- 7 kings

Yod-Zayin (17)

The Yod-Zayin pictographs display a powerful image of "divine victory" when their numbers and meanings are combined to create the number seventeen. The combination reveals, "the crowned man with a sword raised in victory and praise." Seventeen is the image of a triumphant Christ, who swallows up the enemies of death and hell.

It is no surprise many critical events representing God's victory, His promises, deliverance and redemption, occur repeatedly on the seventeenth day of Nisan. Nisan, the month of new beginnings ordained by God, is the appointed time of the Messiah's ultimate mission. On the seventeenth of this new month, the crowned man Jesus, who connects Heaven with Earth, has overcome the curse of Adam by His death on the cross and resurrection from the grave.

Chapter 3: The Meaning of Seventeen

Seventeen in the Bible:

With its powerful imagery, there are many interesting events associated with the number seventeen in the bible. The following are just a few scriptures in which seventeen is referenced:

- **The world-wide flood began on the 17th day** of the month. (Genesis 7:11)
- **Noah's Ark rested on the 17th day** of the month. (Genesis 8:4)
- **Joseph was 17 years old when he was sold** into slavery. (Genesis 37:2)
- **Jacob lived 17 years in Egypt.** (Genesis 47:28)
- **The Ten Commandments were given in 17 verses.** (Exodus 20:1-17)
- **There were 17 Judges from Joshua to King Saul:** Othniel, Ehud, Shamgar, Deborah, Barak, Gideon, Tola, Jair, Jephthah, Ibzan, Elon, Abdon, Samson, Eli, Samuel, Joel, and Abiah.
- **17 people groups/nations were present at the Pentecost and received the Holy Spirit:** Galilee, Parthians, Medes, Elamites, peoples Mesopotamia, Judaea, Cappadocia, Pontus, Asia, Phrygia, Pamphylia, Egypt, Libya, Cyrene, Rome, Cretans and Arabs. (Acts 2:7-11)
- There are **17 things listed that cannot separate us from the love of Jesus:** tribulation, distress, persecution, famine, nakedness, peril, sword, death,

life, angels, principalities, things present, things to come, powers, height, depth, or any other creature. (Romans 8:35-39)

Additionally, many significant events occur on the seventeenth verse or seventeenth chapter in many books of the Bible. It is interesting to note every major covenant between God and mankind in the Bible is listed in either the 17th verse or 17th chapter: **Adam, Noah, Abraham, Moses and the 10 Commandments, King David, and Messiah**. If one examines the totality of the seventeenth verse and chapter for books in the Bible, combined they provide a complete image of the gospel message.

    From the Fall of Adam, to the flood of Noah, to the covenant with Abraham, to the Mosaic Law from Mt. Sinai, to Saul the first king of Israel, to David killing Goliath, to God's covenant with King David for Messiah, many the prophetic images of Christ, to the fulfillment of prophecies in Jesus in the New Testament, to the power of faith, to the outpouring of the Holy Spirit, to the Rapture, to the temporary reign of the Beast and judgment of the world, to the New Heavens and New Earth and the beautiful Bride of Christ, the message of God's redeeming work is clearly written on the number seventeen in either verse or chapter.

    Knowing at the time these scriptures were written there were no divisions delineating chapters or verses, only God in His omniscience could have foreseen the future numbering system and devised His story to be highlighted repeatedly on the seventeenth number throughout the entire Bible.

Chapter 3: The Meaning of Seventeen

Below are some of the major biblical events that occur on the seventeenth number symbolizing God's promises and ultimate victory:

- **Genesis 2:17** – God warned Adam, "but of the tree of the knowledge of good and evil, thou shall not eat of it: for in the day that that eatest thereof thou shalt surely die."
- **Genesis 3:17** – God rebuked Adam for eating of the tree and cursed the ground.
- **Genesis 6:17** – God warns Noah of the coming worldwide flood.
- **Genesis 7:17** – The Ark was lifted up on the floodwaters.
- **Genesis 8:17** – The command from God to leave the Ark.
- **Genesis 9:17** – The "rainbow" covenant of God.
- **Genesis 15:17** – God appears to seal the covenant with Abram.
- **Genesis 17:1** – God made a covenant with Abram, changing Abram's name to Abraham. Prophetic promise of Christ.
- **Genesis 20:17** – First mention of healing by prayer of faith.
- **Genesis 22:17** – Prophetic promise of Christ to Abraham.
- **Exodus 3:17** – God promised to bring Israel out of Egypt to the land flowing with milk and honey.
- **Exodus 16:17** – First day manna was given to Israel.

- **Exodus 17** – Israel traveled and was thirsty. God by the hand of Moses struck a rock and brought forth water out in Horeb. Prophetic of Christ.
- **Exodus 19:17** – Moses brought forth the people of Israel to meet with God at Mt Sinai.
- **Exodus 25:17** – First mention of the Mercy Seat.
- **Exodus 40:17** – The Tabernacle was finished and erected.
- **Numbers 17** – Aaron's rod budding above all the other rods showing God's authority over man's rebellion. This rod is one of three items inside the Ark under the Mercy Seat.
- **Numbers 24:17** – Prophecy of Christ – Star of Jacob.
- **Deuteronomy 9:17** – Moses breaks the tablets of stone written by God: 10 Commandments.
- **Deuteronomy 17** – The promise of Messiah, the coming Prophet like Moses is given.
- **1 Samuel 9:17** – First king of Israel revealed.
- **1 Samuel 17** – The story of David and Goliath.
- **1 Kings 17** – 1st person ever raised from the dead.
- **2 Kings 17** – Israel is taken captive by Assyria.
- **1 Chronicles 17** – God's Covenant with David: Prophecy of Messiah's kingdom and lineage.
- **2 Chronicles 29:17** – Sanctification of the Temple under King Hezekiah.
- **Esther 2:17** – Esther is made Queen.

- **Psalm 117** – Shortest chapter in the Bible. It is also exactly in the middle of all the chapters in the bible.
- **Isaiah 65:17** – The promise of the New Heavens and New Earth, forgetting of the old pain and problems.
- **Jeremiah 17** – Blessedness for the man who trusts in the Lord.
- **Jonah 1:17** – God prepares the great fish to swallow Jonah, and he is in the belly of the fish 3 days and 3 nights. Prophetic of Christ.
- **Zechariah 9:17** – The goodness of the Messiah.
- **Matthew 3:17** – God speaks from heaven, "This is my beloved Son, in whom I am well pleased."
- **Matthew 4:17** – Jesus preached and said, "Repent: for the kingdom of heaven is at hand."
- **Matthew 5:17** – Jesus said, "Think not that I am come to destroy the law, or the prophets: I am not come to destroy, but to fulfill."
- **Matthew 8:17** – Fulfillment of Isaiah's prophecy that Jesus took our infirmities and bare our sicknesses.
- **Matthew 12:17** – Fulfillment of Isaiah's prophecy Jesus is Messiah.
- **Matthew 17** – The Transfiguration.
- **Mark 16:17** – Signs that follow believers of Jesus.
- **John 1:17** - For the law was given by Moses, but grace and truth came by Jesus Christ.
- **John 17** – Jesus prays for believers: His disciples and those to come in the future.

- **Acts 2:17** – Prophecy of Joel for the Last Days and the gift of the Holy Spirit.
- **Acts 8:17** – Peter and John lay hands on Samaritan believers, and they receive the gift of the Holy Spirit.
- **Acts 9:17** – Ananias lays hands on Paul for healing and for him to receive the Holy Spirit.
- **Acts 11:17** – Peter testifies that the gentiles have received the gift of the Holy Spirit.
- **Romans 1:17** – "The just shall live by faith."
- **Romans 5:17** – For if by one man's offence death reigned by one; much more they which receive abundance of grace and of the gift of righteousness shall reign in life by one, Jesus Christ.
- **Romans 10:17** – Faith comes by hearing, and hearing by the word of Christ.
- **1 Corinthians 6:17** – He that is joined to the Lord is one spirit.
- **1 Corinthians 15:17** – If Christ is not raised from the dead, your faith is in vain and you are still in your sins.
- **2 Corinthians 3:17** – Where the Spirit of the Lord is there is liberty.
- **2 Corinthians 5:17** – If any man be in Christ, he is a new creature.
- **Galatians 5:17** – The Flesh and the Spirit war against each other.
- **Colossians 1:17** – Jesus is before all things, and by Him all things consist.

- **1 Thessalonians 4:17** – The Rapture
- **Hebrews 7:17** – Jesus is a priest forever after the order of Melchizedek.
- **Hebrews 10:17** – "Their sins and iniquities I will remember no more," says God.
- **James 2:17** – Even so faith, if it hath not works, is dead, being alone.
- **1 Peter 4:17** – Judgment begins in the House of God.
- **1 John 2:17** – The world will pass away but those who do the will of God remain forever.
- **1 John 4:17** – In Christ our love made perfect; we may have boldness on the day of judgment: because as Jesus is, so are we in this world.
- **Revelation 12:17** – Satan making war with Israel and Christians.
- **Revelations 13:17** – The mark of the Beast.
- **Revelation 16:17** – The final wrath of God poured out.
- **Revelations 22:17** – And the Spirit and the bride say, Come. And let him that hears say, Come. And let him that is thirsty come. And whosoever will, let him take.

Chapter 4
Noah and The Ark

God often uses the Principle of First Mention to introduce a theme, which He later expounds upon in other parables. Each theme reinforces or builds upon the last, revealing a deeper truth. God desires us to see the revelation of Jesus, as the Christ. Just like the Hebrew imagery for the number seventeen, the themes associated with the seventeenth of Nisan represent Jesus and are salvation, deliverance, redemption, and new beginnings.

The first mention of Nisan 17 occurs in the Book of Genesis. By the ninth chapter of the Book of Genesis, the world was completely corrupted from the sin of Adam and Eve eating from the Tree of the Knowledge of Good and Evil. Their rebellion and fallen sinful nature had been passed on to their children and grandchildren. All the people of the world were corrupted; sin impacted the entire planet.

God planned a worldwide flood to deal with the evil of mankind. However, before the flood would be unleashed on Earth, God granted mercy to mankind and other life on the planet, saving by faith those who would trust in Him. As God looked over the earth, the Bible records, "Noah found grace in the eyes of the Lord" Genesis 6:8.

Chapter 4: Noah and The Ark

God warned Noah of the impending flood and provided 120 years for mankind to repent, during which time Noah built the Ark. Unfortunately, few believed in God's impending apocalypse. Only Noah, his wife, their three sons, and their sons' wives believed God and entered the Ark. Finally, the Bible records the day of the catastrophic flood occurred:

"$_{11}$In the six hundredth year of Noah's life, in the second month, the seventeenth day of the month, the same day were all the fountains of the great deep broken up, and the windows of the heaven were opened. $_{12}$And the rain was upon the earth forty days and forty nights."
Genesis 7:11-12

As noted in Chapter 2 of this book, the second month in the Book of Genesis would correspond to the Jewish month Heshvan on the Civil Calendar. Heshvan paralleled the months of October and November depending on the lunar cycle of that year.

The Bible also records the waters of the flood prevailed upon the earth until every square inch of land was covered, Genesis 7:19. The flood was not only exceedingly deep, but it lasted for such an extended period of time that all flesh living on dry land died. The only survivors of this cataclysmic flood were the eight people of Noah's family and the animals God had brought into the Ark.

The last verse in chapter seven of Genesis records the waters of the flood prevailed one hundred and fifty days. Chapter eight of Genesis reveals that Noah's Ark rested on Mt. Ararat long before the waters of the earth had completely receded.

"₄And the ark rested in the seventh month, on the seventeenth day of the month, upon the mountains of Ararat."
Genesis 8:4

Because this event occurred in the Book of Genesis, the calculation of time would be based on the Jewish Civil Calendar. The first month on the Civil Calendar would be Tishri, and the seventh month would correspond to Nisan. Therefore, Noah's Ark rested on Nisan 17th.

Noah's Ark resting upon Mount Ararat was a symbolic portrait of the redemption of mankind and the world from the wrath of God. God's wrath, depicted by the floodwaters, subsided after being poured out on the world. Finally after five long months, the Ark found rest on the mountains of Ararat, even though waters still covered the majority of the Earth. The Hebrew word translated as "Ararat" literally means, "the curse reversed."[1] Thus, the Ark resting on Nisan 17th is a portrait of mankind finding rest after the curse of God's wrath against sin, represented by the flood, was reversed. This theme of "reversing of the curse" on Nisan 17 was prophetic of the future work of the Messiah, who would reverse Adam's curse and the wrath of God later on this same date.

Additionally, the Ark finding reprieve from the floodwaters on Mt. Ararat on Nisan 17th represented a new beginning. The day the Ark rested on a mountain top foreshadowed the first land on which Noah and his family would step on exiting the Ark to begin their new life in a new world.

Chapter 5
Moses and the Red Sea Crossing

The themes of deliverance from evil and wrath as well as new beginnings displayed in the story of Noah's Ark are further developed in the Passover and exodus story of Israel. The story of Moses leading the children of Israel across the Red Sea dominates children's Bible stories. This epic tale has been recreated several times in Hollywood movies. There is not a Christian or Jew who hasn't heard of this famous event in the Bible. While the timing of Moses' crossing is not clearly stated in the Bible as conclusively as Noah's Ark resting on Mt. Ararat, the timeline of events in the Book of Exodus upon evaluation reveals this date was also on Nisan 17th.

Numbers 33:3 declares that the children of Israel were released from Egyptian bondage and began their journey to freedom on the morning of Nisan 15th.

> "$_3$And they departed from Rameses **in the first month, on the fifteenth day of the first month**; on the morrow after the Passover the children of Israel went out with an high hand in the sight of all the Egyptians."
> Numbers 33:3

The timeline for Pharaoh's release occurred sometime after midnight but before the dawn on Nisan 15th, as scripture reports in verse 31 that Pharaoh called for Moses and Aaron by night. Therefore, we can be certain Israel left on the morning of Nisan 15th before sunrise.

> "29And it came to pass, that **at midnight the Lord smote all the firstborn** in the land of Egypt, from the firstborn of Pharaoh that sat on his throne unto the firstborn of the captive that was in the dungeon; and all the firstborn of cattle. 30And Pharaoh rose up in the night, he, and all his servants, and all the Egyptians; and there was a great cry in Egypt; for there was not a house where there was not one dead. 31And **he [Pharaoh] called for Moses and Aaron by night**, and said, **Rise up, and get you forth from among my people,** both ye and the children of Israel; and go, serve the Lord, as ye have said. 32**Also take your flocks and your herds, as ye have said, and be gone**; and bless me also. 33And **the Egyptians were urgent upon the people, that they might send them out of the land in haste**; for they said, We be all dead men."
> Exodus 12:29-33

Additionally, we know Israel left Egypt immediately after Pharaoh released them and their animals. The words "in haste" in Exodus verse 33 above literally meant, "promptly." According to verse 39, the Jews did not wait around in Egypt after Pharaoh's release but were "thrust out," which literally was "to be driven out from the land." The Egyptians feared the God of Israel after the last plague and believed if any Israeli remained in the land, all the remaining Egyptians would die.

> "$_{39}$And they baked unleavened cakes of the dough which they brought forth out of Egypt, for it was not leavened; because **they were thrust out of Egypt, and could not tarry**, neither had they prepared for themselves any victual."
> Exodus 12:39

Therefore upon receiving the edict to vacate Egypt by Pharaoh, Israel left quickly, early in the morning of Nisan 15th before the sun had even risen. It is interesting to note that Israel was released from Egyptian bondage on the very same day they entered it 430 years earlier under the protection of Joseph.

> "And it came to pass at the end of the four hundred and thirty years, even the selfsame day it came to pass, that all the hosts of the Lord went out from the land of Egypt."
> Exodus 12:41

The Exodus story is very detailed regarding the route Israel traveled and the duration of their journey. The details of their route and camp at night establish a clear timeline.

> "$_{17}$And it came to pass, when Pharaoh had let the people go, that God led them not through the way of the land of the Philistines, although that was near; for God said, Lest peradventure the people repent when

they see war, and they return to Egypt: ₁₈But God led the people about, through the way of the wilderness of the Red sea: and the children of Israel went up harnessed out of the land of Egypt. ₁₉And Moses took the bones of Joseph with him: for he had straitly sworn the children of Israel, saying, God will surely visit you; and ye shall carry up my bones away hence with you. ₂₀**And they took their journey from Succoth, and encamped in E'-tham, in the edge of the wilderness.** ₂₁And the Lord went before them by day in a pillar of a cloud, to lead them the way; and by night in a pillar of fire, to give them light; to go by day and night: ₂₂He took not away the pillar of the cloud by day, nor the pillar of fire by night, from before the people."
Exodus 13:17-22

After leaving Egypt, Israel traveled toward E'tham. Later that evening (which began Nisan 16th) Israel camped in E'-tham for the night. Scripture continued to clarify that God led the children the next day toward Pi-ha-hi'-roth near Ba'al-ze'-phon. This "day" of travel would also be on Nisan 16th. God also spoke directly to Moses to inform him He was going to harden Pharaoh's heart to come after Israel.

"₁And the Lord spake unto Moses, saying, ₂Speak unto the children of Israel, **that they turn and encamp before Pi-ha-hi'-roth, between Mig'-dol and the sea, over against Ba'-al-ze'-phon**: before it shall ye encamp by the sea. ₃For Pharaoh will say of the children of Israel, They are entangled in the land, the wilderness hath shut them in. ₄And I will harden

Pharaoh's heart, that he shall follow after them; and I will be honored upon Pharaoh, and upon all his host; that the Egyptians may know that I am the Lord. And they did so."
Exodus 14:1-4

As the children of Israel traveled toward Pi-ha-hi'-roth to camp for the second night, Pharaoh's heart was changed toward them. Then Pharaoh ordered his army to pursue after Israel and destroy them. Pharaoh's army left Egypt on Nisan 16th during the day while Israel was journeying to Pi-ha-hiroth. By late afternoon on Nisan 16th, Pharaoh's army had almost caught up with the children of Israel. The people panicked seeing the dust from the chariots. Moses reassured them to not fear for God would fight for them.

"$_8$And the Lord hardened the heart of Pharaoh king of Egypt, and he pursued after the children of Israel: and the children of Israel went out with a high hand. $_9$But **the Egyptians pursued after them**, all the horses and chariots of Pharaoh, and his horsemen, and his army, and **overtook them encamping by the sea**, beside Pihahiroth, before Baalzephon. $_{10}$And when Pharaoh drew nigh, the children of Israel lifted up their eyes, and, behold, the Egyptians marched after them; and they were sore afraid: and the children of Israel cried out unto the Lord. $_{11}$And they said unto Moses, Because there were no graves in Egypt, hast thou taken us away to die in the wilderness? wherefore hast thou dealt thus with us, to carry us forth out of Egypt? $_{12}$Is not this the word that we did tell thee in Egypt, saying, Let us alone, that we may serve the Egyptians? For it had been better for us to serve the Egyptians, than that we should die in the wilderness. ₁₃And Moses said unto the people, Fear ye not, stand still, and see the salvation of the Lord, which he will shew to you today: for the Egyptians whom ye have seen to day, ye shall see them again no more forever. ₁₄The Lord shall fight for you, and ye shall hold your peace." Exodus 14:8-14

As Pharaoh's army approached, the angel of the Lord was described as a pillar of cloud, indicating this event began during the daylight hours. Exodus 13:21-22 describes the difference between the pillar of the cloud and pillar of fire, indicating the cloud pillar was for daytime travel and the fiery pillar was for nocturnal assurance. In Exodus 14:19, the pillar of a cloud went from before the camp of Israel to behind them. The cloud stood between Pharaoh's army and the children of Israel. This *"pillar of a cloud"* is later described in Exodus 14:20 as giving light unto Israel but darkness unto Pharaoh. The pillar stood between the two enemy camps all night. Therefore, we see the timeline depicted by the angelic pillar of cloud and fire indicates Pharaoh's army originally approached during the day time on Nisan 16th and transitioned to the pillar of fire later that night to give light to Israel on Nisan 17th.

"₁₅And the Lord said unto Moses, Wherefore criest thou unto me? speak unto the children of Israel, that they go forward: ₁₆But lift thou up thy rod, and stretch out thine hand over the sea, and divide it: and the children of Israel shall go on dry ground through the

Chapter 5: Moses and the Red Sea Crossing

midst of the sea. ₁₇And I, behold, I will harden the hearts of the Egyptians, and they shall follow them: and I will get me honor upon Pharaoh, and upon all his host, upon his chariots, and upon his horsemen. ₁₈And the Egyptians shall know that I am the Lord, when I have gotten me honor upon Pharaoh, upon his chariots, and upon his horsemen. ₁₉And ***the angel of God, which went before the camp of Israel, removed and went behind them; and the pillar of the cloud went from before their face, and stood behind them***: ₂₀***And it came between the camp of the Egyptians and the camp of Israel; and it was a cloud and darkness to them, but it gave light by night to these: so that the one came not near the other <u>all the night</u>.***"
Exodus 14:15-20

Later that night on Nisan 17th, Moses stretched out his hand over the Red Sea. The Lord produced a night wind to blow, causing the sea floor to dry. The English words **"all that night"** in Exodus 14:21 are translated from a single Hebrew word, "layil," which literally means, "night." Therefore, the wind was not blowing "all night long." Instead, the correct translation should be, a "night wind" blew and divided the waters and dried the land beneath them.

"₂₁And Moses stretched out his hand over the sea; and the Lord caused the sea to go back by ***a strong east wind all that night***, and made the sea dry land, and the waters were divided. ₂₂***And the children of Israel went into the midst of the sea upon the dry*** *ground*: and the waters were a wall unto them on their right hand, and on their left. ₂₃**And the Egyptians pursued, and went in after them to the midst of the sea,** even all Pharaoh's horses, his chariots, and his horsemen. ₂₄And it came to pass, that **in the morning watch** the Lord looked unto the host of the Egyptians **through the pillar of fire and of the cloud,** and troubled the host of the Egyptians, ₂₅And took off their chariot wheels, that they drave them heavily: so that the Egyptians said, Let us flee from the face of Israel; for the Lord fighteth for them against the Egyptians. ₂₆And the Lord said unto Moses, Stretch out thine hand over the sea, that the waters may come again upon the Egyptians, upon their chariots, and upon their horsemen. ₂₇**And Moses stretched forth his hand over the sea, and the sea returned to his strength <u>when the morning appeared</u>;** and the Egyptians fled against it; and the Lord overthrew the Egyptians in the midst of the sea. ₂₈And the waters returned, and covered the chariots, and the horsemen, and all the host of Pharaoh that came into the sea after them; there remained not so much as one of them. ₂₉But the children of Israel walked upon dry land in the midst of the sea; and the waters were a wall unto them on their right hand, and on their left. ₃₀Thus the Lord saved Israel that day out of the hand of the Egyptians; and Israel saw the Egyptians dead upon the sea shore."

Exodus 14:21-30

Sometime between sunset and dawn, Israel crossed over the sea. Understanding the original Hebrew words for our English translations in the Exodus story helps clarify the timeline of the verses regarding the children of Israel crossing the Red Sea. Pharaoh's army followed Israel into the Read Sea, and the Lord saw the events at "the morning watch." These three events occur on the night of Nisan 17.

The Jews divided the night into three periods of time for military watches. Each watch represented four hours of time, with the morning watch corresponding to the hours between 2:00 AM until sunrise.[2] Therefore, the Exodus story records precisely the time the Egyptians were in the Red Sea attempting to cross on dry land, pursuing after the Israelites, who had already successfully crossed. The Lord looked from Heaven in verse 24 during "the morning watch" and saw Pharaoh's army pursuing Israel. This means Pharaoh's army crossed the sea between 2 AM and sunrise.

God instructed Moses to wave his hand over the waters to close the opening in the sea, thus drowning Pharaoh's army. In verse 27, Moses "stretched forth his hand over the sea, and the sea returned to his strength **_when the morning appeared_**." The English words for the phrase *"when the morning"* consist of only one Hebrew word, "boqer," which means, "dawn." The Hebrew word translated "appeared" is the word "panah," which means, "dawning" or "to appear." The Hebrew phrasing portrays an image of Moses stretching forth his hand on the morning of Nisan 17th just as daybreak was occurring, before the sun was above the horizon.

Pharaoh's army perished forever with the rising of the sun, redeeming Israel from the bondage and fear of the strength of the Egyptian army. The morning of Nisan 17th becomes a day of new beginnings for the nation of Israel as free men. No longer are they slaves to Egypt. All that Egypt represented to Israel: its power, influence, and dominion over them, died with Pharaoh's army in the Red Sea. God had personally redeemed them with a mighty hand. Yahweh brought miraculous deliverance and a new life for the children of Israel on Nisan 17th just before sunrise.

Chapter 6
Joshua and the First Fruits

The Book of Joshua opens with the children of Israel preparing to enter Canaan, the Promised Land, after the death of Moses. In chapter three, Israel miraculously crosses the Jordan River during the time of spring flooding. When the priests carrying the Ark of the Covenant step into the river, God divides the waters and allows Israel to walk across on dry land. Upon entering the Promised Land, God reminded Joshua that Israel had forsaken His covenant in the wilderness. According to the Abrahamic covenant, all the males were to be circumcised. While camping at Gil'-gal, Joshua ordered all Israeli males circumcised to fulfill covenant law and granted a period of time for healing. While at Gil'-gal, Israel kept the Passover for the third time recorded in Scripture. The first mention of the observance of Passover was in Egypt (Exodus chapter 12). The second record is in Numbers chapter 9 verses 1-5. The Book of Joshua contains the third account:

"$_{10}$And the children of Israel encamped in Gil'-gal, and kept the Passover on the fourteenth day of the month at evening in the plains of Jericho. $_{11}$And they did eat of the old grain of the land on the morrow

after the Passover, unleavened cakes, and parched grain in the selfsame day. ₁₂And the man'-na ceased on the morrow after they had eaten of the old grain of the land; neither had the children of Israel man'-na anymore; but they did eat of the fruit of the land of Canaan that year."
Joshua 5:10-12

Not only does this passage provide the third account of the Passover, but it also gives the exact timeline for the disappearance of Heavenly manna. The record indicates manna stopped on the morning of the 16th of Nisan. The reason for the significance of the date the manna ceased was to highlight the day in which the children of God first ate from the new grain of the Promised Land. In order to properly determine the timeline to know exactly which day the manna ceased, we will examine every aspect of the Scriptures. It is also important to remember Israel ate manna continually from the time it was first given in the wilderness until the day it stopped: "And the children of Israel did eat man'-na forty years" (Exodus 16:35). The only exception in the daily provision of manna by God was for a Sabbath:

> "²⁵And Moses said, Eat that today; for today is a Sabbath unto the Lord: today ye shall not find it [manna] in the field. ²⁶Six days ye shall gather it [manna]; but on the seventh day, the Sabbath, in it there shall be none."
> Exodus 16:25-26

Chapter 6: Joshua and the First Fruits

The timeline of events surrounding the third Passover begins in Joshua chapter five verse ten, which explains Israel kept the Passover on Nisan 14th. The phrase "kept the Passover" signified Israel killed the Passover lamb in accordance with Mosaic Law on the fourteenth of Nisan in the evening. Israel received manna on the morning of Nisan 14th. The Passover lamb was killed in the evening of the fourteenth and consumed later that night on Nisan 15th in accordance with Mosaic Law.

Scripture notes in chapter five, verse eleven that Israel ate unleavened bread prepared from old grain of the land of Canaan on the day after the Passover, which is Nisan 15th. Nisan 15th is the date for the Feast of Unleavened Bread. The Israelites probably found old grain in Canaan storehouses when they entered the land several days earlier. The reason Israel had to eat old grain or unleavened bread was because of the absence of manna on Nisan 15th. At first the absence of manna on Nisan 15th is not obvious until one remembers the Lord does not send manna on His Sabbath days. Nisan 15th is a High Sabbath, or Annual Feast Day Sabbath. While it is not the weekly Sabbath (Saturday), Nisan 15th is the Sabbath of the Lord given in Leviticus during the wilderness. Therefore, because of the Sabbath, Israel would not have received manna to eat in the morning of Nisan 15. They would have been forced to eat old grain as unleavened bread for breakfast, since it was forbidden to eat any new grain until after the Feast of First Fruits had been presented to the Lord.

"$_{10}$Speak unto the children of Israel, and say unto them, When ye be come into the land which I give unto you, and shall reap the harvest thereof, then ye shall bring a sheaf of the first fruits of your harvest unto the priest: ₁₁And he shall wave the sheaf before the Lord, to be accepted for you on the morrow after the Sabbath the priest shall wave it... ₁₄And ye shall eat neither bread, nor parched grain, nor green ears, until the self-same day that ye have brought an offering unto your God: it shall be a statute for ever throughout your generations in all your dwellings." Leviticus 23:10-14

Examining events from strictly a Pharisaical viewpoint, the earliest day the Feast of First Fruits could occur was on Nisan 16th. However, in Joshua 5:12, scripture states on the day **after** Israel had eaten old grain from the land (Nisan 15th), the manna ceased. That means on the day after Nisan 15th, on Nisan 16, the manna stopped. Taking a literal interpretation of the Scriptures, if manna did not fall on Nisan 16th, then the last day manna would have been given to Israel would have been Nisan 14th. However, the Scripture affirms manna was given the day after they ate of the old grain, which was the day after Passover. Therefore, on the Sabbath day of Nisan 15th the children of Israel ate old grain as their unleavened bread (Joshua 5:11).

Since we know from Joshua 5:12 manna ceased on the day after the fifteenth of Nisan, the last day for manna to have been given must have occurred on Nisan 16th. Israel never ate manna after Nisan 16. The next morning was Nisan 17th, and the children of Israel kept the Feast of First Fruits. After the new grain was sacrificed to God during the morning of Feast of First Fruits, the Israelites could eat new grain and fruits of the land. This means on Nisan 17th,

Israel ate the fresh grain of the Promised Land because there was no more manna given by God (verse 12). The chart below provides a time outline of biblical events in the Book of Joshua, chapter five.

Days of Manna

Chart 4

	Nisan 14	**Nisan 15**	**Nisan 16**	**Nisan 17**
Morning	**Passover** Manna Given Passover lamb killed before evening (v.10)	**High Sabbath** No Manna Given Exodus 16:25 Eat old grain of the land (v.11)	Last Day Manna Given (v. 12)	No Manna Given Eat First Fruits of the Promised Land
	Nisan 15 **High Sabbath**	**Nisan 16**	**Nisan 17**	**Nisan 18**
Evening	Passover eaten with unleavened bread (v. 11)	Eat old grain of the land (v.11)		

While Israel had already entered the Land of Promise days before, they still did not have the authority to eat of the fullness of land, which was the fulfillment of God's vowed blessing. By eating from the new grain on Nisan 17th, Israel finally experienced the fulfillment of God's promises of bountiful provisions in the land overflowing with milk and honey.

There is a spiritual analogy accompanying the eating of new fruit of the land as well. The Jews had finally entered into God's rest and provision. No longer are they strangers wandering in the wilderness with nothing to call their own. The land before Israel now belonged to them. All the fruits therein were theirs to eat freely. This imagery is reminiscent of the Garden of Eden, which belonged to God, yet Adam was given free reign to eat of the abundance of fruit, with one exception. The imagery of eating from the Promised Land on Nisan 17th can also be spiritually symbolic of the future promises given to all God's children. Jesus stated all who eat of the Bread of Heaven will obtain entrance into the Kingdom of God, where there is abundance to meet their every need.

Chapter 7
Hezekiah and The Temple

During the time of the divided kingdoms of Israel and Judah, many evil kings arose in the land. A succession of evil kings ruled generation after generation. During their reign, idolatry and false gods replaced the true worship of Yahweh (Jehovah). Even the glorious temple built by Solomon was vandalized and overrun with idols. King Ahaz, the father of Hezekiah, was so evil that he robbed the treasury of the House of the Lord. Ahaz took all its gold and silver as a bribe to the King of Assyria to help protect Judah from an invading army. King Ahaz also removed the brazen altar, the laver, and destroyed many of the articles in the Lord's Temple, worshipping false idols. Eventually, King Ahaz dismissed the Levites and closed the Temple doors permanently, setting up idols to worship instead (2 Kings chapter 16). As a result of the promotion of false gods and idols, most of the inhabitants of Judah were spiritually deceived, and many followed after the king's folly. The Levitical priesthood also became "unclean" when the Levites stopped ministering before the Lord and could no longer offer sacrifices for their sins according to the Mosaic Law.

After King Ahaz died, his son Hezekiah became king over Judah. Hezekiah was recorded as a righteous man, who did "good" in the eyes of the Lord. The twenty-ninth chapter of the Book of 2 Chronicles outlines events during the reign of King Hezekiah. King Hezekiah immediately began to repair the spiritual and physical damage his father performed in the land, specifically regarding the treatment of the House of God, Solomon's Temple. In the first year of his reign, Hezekiah opened the doors of the Temple and repaired them (2 Chronicles 29:3). He also gathered the Levites and priests, instructing them to sanctify themselves and the House of God (verses 4-17). Hezekiah's goal was to restore the true worship of Yahweh to the Land of Israel. Notice the Scripture states these events took place in the first month, which is Nisan.

> "₁₅And they *[the Levites]* gathered their brethren, and sanctified themselves, and came, according to the commandment of the king *[King Hezekiah]*, by the words of the LORD, to cleanse the house of the LORD. ₁₆And the priests went into the inner part of the house of the LORD, to cleanse it, and brought out all the uncleanness that they found in the temple of the LORD into the court of the house of the LORD. And the Levites took it, to carry it out abroad into the brook Ki'-dron. ₁₇Now they began **on the first day of the first month** to sanctify, and on the eighth day of the month came they to the porch of the LORD: so they sanctified the house of the LORD in eight days; and **in the sixteenth day of the first month they made an end**."
> 2 Chronicles 29:20

Chapter 7: Hezekiah and The Temple

The sanctification of the priests and the Levites took eight days. The cleansing and sanctification of the Temple took another eight days, totaling sixteen days for purification. On Nisan 16th, the Levites finally finished the cleansing, repairs, and purification necessary for Temple worship to resume the next day. The priests reported to King Hezekiah (in verse eighteen) they had finished cleaning the entire House of God, restoring the vessels for worship, and the altar for burnt offerings. On the morning of Nisan 17th, King Hezekiah rose early, gathered the children of Israel, and resumed temple worship for the first time in many years. They began worship with sin offerings, making atonement for the nation Israel's past sins of idolatry.

"$_{20}$Then Hez-e-ki'-ah the king rose early, and gathered the rules of the city, and went up to the house of the LORD."
2 Chronicles 29:20

The imagery associated with the English words translated as *"rose early"* when considering the same Hebrew words translated in other places in the Bible provides the understanding that the king was rising long before dawn. The matter before Hezekiah was of such significant importance that he could not wait until the sunrise to begin. Thus, King Hezekiah and the rulers of the city came before the Temple of Yahweh on Nisan 17th. Before the sunrise, sacrifices of seven were to make atonement for the people of the Kingdom of Judah. Seven represents the number symbolic of completion. Thus, with the dawning sun, true worship is completely restored to God's people and the land of Israel on Nisan 17th.

53

Chapter 8

Esther and Deliverance from Death

The Book of Esther is an interesting book, because it is the only book in the entire Bible where the name of Yahweh is not mentioned directly. Yet, even though God's name is not mentioned, God is still at work behind the scenes ruling in the great Persian Empire and nation of Israel. In the story, Ha'man, the enemy of Israel, served as a type of antichrist. Ha'man, whose pride was injured by a Jew, devised a plan to annihilate all the Jews in retaliation. He deceived King Ahasuerus into believing there was a group of people within the kingdom who were essentially lawless, not abiding by or respecting the king's laws. Ha'man convinced the king to allow him to act on his behalf and ordered the annihilation of the Jews in the Persian Empire to confiscate of their wealth. Ha'man's plan is carried out on Nisan 13th when a decree is announced for the future destruction of Israelites in the month of Adar throughout all the Persian Empire.

"$_8$And Ha'man said unto King Ahasuerus, There is a certain people scattered abroad and dispersed among the people in all the provinces of thy kingdom; and their laws are diverse from all people; neither keep they the king's laws: therefore it is not for the

Chapter 8: Ester and Deliverance from Death

king's profit to suffer them. ₉If it please the king, **let it be written that they [Israelites] may be destroyed:** and I will pay ten thousand talents of silver to the hands of those that have the charge of the business, to bring it into the king's treasuries. ₁₀And the king took his ring from his hand, and gave it unto **Ha'man** the son of Hammedatha the Agagite, **the Jews' enemy**. ₁₁And the king said unto Ha'man, The silver is given to thee, the people also, to do with them as it seemeth good to thee. ₁₂Then were the king's scribes called **on the thirteenth day of the first month**, and there was written according to all that Ha'man had commanded unto the king's lieutenants, and to the governors that were over every province, and to the rulers of every people of every province according to the writing thereof, and to every people after their language; in the name of King Ahasuerus was it written, and sealed with the king's ring."
Esther 3:8-12

Of interesting note, in his betrayal of the Jewish nation, silver was given as a reward to those who will conspire to kill the Jews and take their wealth into the king's treasury. This betrayal in exchange for silver imagery is prophetic of events seen in the New Testament on the same date. On Nisan 13th, Judas Iscariot betrayed Jesus for thirty (30) pieces of silver. In response to Ha'man's decree, the entire nation of Israel began to mourn, and unknown to Ha'man, Queen Esther was a Jew.

Esther's uncle, Mordecai, was a scribe who was often found sitting at the king's gates. He had previously thwarted a plan to murder the king, and now sat at the gate learning the news of Israel's future impending doom. Mordecai in despair rips his clothing and seeks audience with the queen to intervene for their nation. Mordecai informed Queen Esther what Ha'man had done and of the publication of Adar 13th being the future date planned for Israel's annihilation. Queen Esther was shocked. Left as the only hope for her people, Esther devised a plan to approach her husband. Approaching the king without being summoned was a violation of Persian law, and Esther could be killed. Esther knew the probability of her death was high; therefore in preparation for her intercessory act, Esther asked Mordecai to instruct all the Jews to fast for three days before she made her appeal.

> "$_{16}$Go, gather together all the Jews that are present in Shushan, and fast ye for me, and **neither eat nor drink three days**, **night or day**: I also and my maidens will fast likewise; **and so will I go in unto the king**, which is not according to the law: and if I perish, I perish."
> Esther 4:16

Three days later on Nisan 16th, Esther risked her life and appeared before King Ahasuerus without being summoned. The king intervened and spared her life, asking what she desired of him. Queen Esther replied, "If it pleases the king, may the king and Ha'man **come this day** to the banquet that I have prepared" (see Esther 5:4). At the banquet on Nisan 16th, the king questioned Esther again as to her desire. At that time, she invited the king and Ha'man to a second banquet the following day. The next day, on

Chapter 8: Ester and Deliverance from Death

Nisan 17th at the second banquet, Queen Esther pleaded the case for the salvation of her people, Israel.

> "₁So the king and Ha'man came to banquet with Esther the queen. ₂And the king said again unto Esther **on the second day** at the banquet of wine, What is thy petition, queen Esther? and it shall be granted thee: and what is thy request? and it shall be performed, even to the half of the kingdom. ₃Then Esther the queen answered and said, If I have found favour in thy sight, O king, and if it please the king, let my life be given me at my petition, and my people at my request: ₄For we are sold, I and my people, to be destroyed, to be slain, and to perish. But if we had been sold for bondmen and bondwomen, I had held my tongue, although the enemy could not countervail the king's damage. ₅Then the king Ahasuerus answered and said unto Esther the queen, Who is he, and where is he, that durst presume in his heart to do so? ₆And Esther said, The adversary and enemy is this wicked Ha'man. Then Ha'man was afraid before the king and the queen. ₇And the king arising from the banquet of wine in his wrath went into the palace garden: and Ha'man stood up to make request for his life to Esther the queen; for he saw that there was evil determined against him by the king. ₈Then the king returned out of the palace garden into the place of the banquet of wine; and Ha'man was fallen upon the bed whereon Esther was. Then said the king, Will he force the queen also before me in the house? As the word went out of king's mouth, they covered Ha'man's face. ₉And Harbonah, one of the

chamberlains, said before the king, Behold also, the gallows fifty cubits high, which Ha'man had made for Mor'de-ca-i, who had spoken good for the king, standeth in the house of Ha'man. Then the king said, Hang him thereon. ₁₀**So they hanged Ha'man** on the gallows that he had prepared for Mor'de-ca-i. Then was the king's wrath pacified."
Esther 7:1-10

As a result of Esther's plea, Ha'man was killed and salvation was granted unto the Jews on Nisan 17th. The king transferred authority from the enemy (Ha'man) to the children of God (represented by Mordecai).

In Persia, the king's decree was absolute. Persian law did not allow for any change to be made to the original decree of a king. It was believed the king was perfect. Therefore, his decrees were perfect and not subject to change. If perchance a change was required, the king must issue another decree that did not legally contradict the first order, essentially allowing for a loophole.

Only another decree of equal perfection could allow the Jews a chance at life. Because King Ahasuerus' original edict (issued under Ha'man) calling for the destruction of the Jews could not be rescinded or reversed, additional letters were sent out authorizing the Jews to assemble to defend themselves with the help of the Persian army on that future date in Adar. The new order also gave them permission to kill their enemies and confiscate their enemies' wealth on Adar 13th. The day originally appointed for Israel's annihilation became the date of their physical redemption.

"₁₁Wherein **the king granted the Jews which were in every city to gather themselves together, and**

to stand for their life, to destroy, to slay and to cause to perish, all the power of the people and province that would assault them, both little ones and women, and to take the spoil of them for a prey. "
Esther 8:11

King Ahasuerus' first decree for death was symbolic of God's law, which is perfect and holy and cannot be reversed by any man. God's law condemned sin, required the death of sinners, and could not be reversed. Similarly, God's punishment of death for sin could not be rescinded by a change in heart. Only another decree, equal in perfection and justice, could be extended to give mankind an escape "loophole" from the death sentence originally issued. Therefore, God issued the decree in which anyone fulfilling His perfect law may become the substitute for other sinners. Now the penalty of death could be legally fulfilled. Ironically, God Himself was the only being capable of completing His new decree. Therefore, He stepped into time and human flesh as Jesus the Christ and fulfilled the Mosaic Law perfectly, becoming the substitution sacrifice for sinners. God's sacrifice allowed the true sinners (humanity) to be released from the punishment of death while still upholding God's justice.

For all practical purposes, the redemption of the Jews occurred on Nisan 17th, when King Ahasuerus' heart towards the Jewish nation changed upon the revelation that Queen Esther was a Hebrew descendent. However, Israel's complete deliverance from physical destruction did not culminate until several months later on Adar 13th, when the king's army rose up to defend the Jews. This theme of salvation, beginning on Nisan 17th yet seemingly delayed for a period of time until the month of Adar, portrays the finished work and ministry of Jesus Christ currently in progress between His resurrection and Second Coming.

Jesus rose from the grave on Nisan 17th and immediately deliverance from sin and death was granted to all who would believe. Believers are spiritually and mentally free at this moment. Yet, an interlude of time remains before the fulfillment of the last enemy, death is destroyed, and when Believers receive their immortal physical bodies. Just as a period of time existed between Nisan 17th to Adar 13th, indicative of the delay between the king's decree of freedom from death and the final date of deliverance, so too it is for Believers who have been freed legally from the enemy of death but still await the final deliverance of their physical bodies.

"$_{21}$For since by man came death, by man also the resurrection of the dead. $_{22}$For as in Adam all die, even so in Christ shall all be made alive. $_{23}$**But every man in his own order: <u>Christ the first fruits</u>; <u>afterwards</u> they that are Christ's at His coming**... $_{25}$For He must reign, till He hath put all enemies under His feet. $_{26}$**The last enemy that shall be destroyed is death.** $_{27}$For he [God] hath put all things under his [Jesus] feet..."
1 Corinthians 15:21-27

"$_{23}$And not only they, but ourselves also which have the first fruits of the Spirit, even we ourselves groan

within ourselves **waiting for** the adoption, **the redemption of our body**."
Romans 8:23

"$_{49}$And as we have borne the image of the earthly, we shall also bear the image of the heavenly. $_{50}$Now this I say brethren, that flesh and blood cannot inherit the kingdom of God; neither doth corruption inherit incorruption. $_{51}$Behold, I show you a mystery; We shall not all die, but we shall all be changed, $_{52}$In a moment, in the twinkling of an eye, at the last trump: for the trumpet shall sound, and the dead shall be raised incorruptible, and we shall be changed. $_{53}$**For this corruption must put on incorruption, and this mortal put on immortality**. $_{54}$So when this corruptible shall have put on incorruption, and this mortal shall have put on immortality, then shall be brought to pass the saying that is written, **Death is swallowed up in victory**."
1 Corinthians 15:49-54

"$_{12}$That we should be to the praise of his glory, who first trusted in Christ. $_{13}$In whom ye also trusted, after that ye heard the word of truth, the gospel of your salvation: in whom also after that ye believed, **ye were sealed with that Holy Spirit** of promise, $_{14}$Which is the earnest of our inheritance <u>**until the redemption**</u> of the purchased possession, unto the praise of his glory."
Ephesians 1:12-14

Chapter 9

The Resurrection of Jesus

Most Christians usually think in terms of Gregorian days regarding the resurrection of Jesus. The only fact they know for certain is that Christ rose from the dead on Sunday morning. This truth is well documented biblically. Yet, it is also true of the particular Sunday that Jesus rose from the dead was on the Jewish date of Nisan 17th, the day of the Feast of First Fruits. Anatolius the Bishop of Laodicea during the third century (269-283 A.D.) was quoted referring to the timing of the resurrection of Jesus being on the Nisan 17th.

> "For, although they lay it down as a thing unlawful, that the beginning of the Paschal festival would be extended so far as to the moon's twentieth; yet they cannot deny that it ought to be extended to the sixteenth and seventeenth, which coincide with the day on which the Lord rose from the dead."[3]

We know from scriptures in the Book of Exodus that the Passover Lamb must be killed on Nisan 14th (in the late afternoon/evening) before Nisan 15th. Therefore, we know that Jesus died on Nisan 14th. The following day was a High Sabbath for the Feast of Unleavened Bread on Nisan

Chapter 9: The Resurrection of Jesus

15th. Jesus was in the grave three days and three nights rising on Nisan 17th, the third day.

There has been a longstanding presumption by Christian scholars that Jesus rose on Nisan 16th. This belief was based upon the premise Nisan 16th was the date for the Feast of First Fruits celebrated on the Jewish calendar. While it is true that since Hillel II the Jewish calendar has maintained a fixed date for the Feast of First Fruits on Nisan 16th, Hillel's calendar did not begin until the Fourth Century.

In biblical times during the life of Jesus, the entire Jewish calendar including the date for the Feast of First Fruits was ordained by the sighting of the first silver of the new moon. The sighting of the moon was reported to the Jewish Sanhedrin, who then began the official counting for the first day of the month. The Sanhedrin was primarily composed of two Jewish religious sects: the Pharisees and the Sadducees. Each sect had a different interpretation of Mosaic scripture in Leviticus 23:11 regarding the method for counting from the Sabbath day to determine the date for the Feast of First Fruits.

> "$_{11}$And he shall wave the sheaf before the Lord, to be accepted for you: **_on the morrow after the Sabbath_** the priest shall wave it."
> Leviticus 23:11

While both sects believed the timing began the day after the Sabbath, the notion of which Sabbath day remained in question. In this particular week of the year, there are two Sabbaths: the High Sabbath and a regular weekly Sabbath. The Pharisees interpreted the word "Sabbath" in this scripture to mean the High Sabbath designated by the Feast of Unleavened Bread on Nisan 15th. Therefore, Pharisees always held the Feast of First Fruits on Nisan 16th. Since Hillel II was a Pharisee, his calendar was based on this pharisaical interpretation of scripture, fixing the Feast of First Fruits to Nisan 16th, which history teaches was the tradition most dominant after 70 AD.

The Sadducees construed the "Sabbath" in Leviticus 23:11 to be referring to the regular weekly Sabbath, which is Friday night to Saturday night. Therefore, the Sadducees believe the Feast of First Fruits would always occur on a Sunday. The Sadducees were the ruling sect during the life of Jesus. According to the Jewish historian Josephus, both Cai'aphas and An-nas, who served in the position of High Priests the year Jesus died, were Sadducees.[4] Therefore, while the current Jewish calendar has a fixed date of Nisan 16th for the Feast of First Fruits, this rule was not in effect the year Jesus died and has no relevance to Christ's crucifixion week.

In the week of Jesus' resurrection, Nisan 17th corresponded to Feast of First Fruits, which occurred on a Sunday as recognized by the Sadducees. As the ruling class for the Temple during the time of Christ, the Sadducee interpretation of the Feast of First Fruits timeline would trump any Pharisaical interpretation we have today for the date for First Fruits. Additionally, if Christ rose on Nisan 16th, there would be no way to acquire three days and three nights of death as foretold by Jesus in Matthew 12:40.

> "[39]But he answered and said unto them, An evil and adulterous generation seeketh after a sign; and there shall no sign be given to it, but the sign of the

prophet Jonas: ₄₀For as Jonah was three days and three nights in the whale's belly; **so shall the Son of man be <u>three days and three nights</u> in the heart of the earth**."
Matthew 12:39-40

Knowing Jesus died on or around 3:00 PM on Nisan 14th, a calculation of the time Jesus would be dead if He rose on Nisan 16th before sunrise would be less than thirty-nine (39) hours. Obviously, thirty-nine (39) hours is nowhere near three days and three nights of death. The following charts compare traditional Church teaching of thirty-nine hours of death with realistic biblical interpretation of sixty-three hours of death. The charts use the Jewish timeline for days in Nisan.

Traditional Church Teaching

Chart 5

	Nisan 14 Jesus dies at 3PM	**Nisan 15** High Sabbath & Weekly Sabbath	**Nisan 16** Jesus alive before sunrise
Day	1st Day Dead	2nd Day Dead	Alive
	Nisan 15	**Nisan 16**	**Nisan 17**
Night	1st Night Dead	2nd Night Dead	Appears to Disciples

In the traditional theory, Jesus died on Nisan 14th called Good Friday and rose on Nisan 16th, Resurrection Sunday. Many Believers holding this theory argue it spans three different Gregorian days: Friday, Saturday and Sunday or Jewish days Nisan 14th, 15th, and 16th. However, if one calculates the periods for death, the maximum amount of time Christ would be dead was thirty-nine hours (39), and only thirty-six hours (36) if calculated from the time of actual entombment.

3:00 PM Nisan 14th to 3:00 PM Nisan 15th = 24 hours
3:00 PM Nisan 15th to 6:00 AM Nisan 16th = <u>15 hours</u>
Total   39 hours

Never in biblical scripture or history has thirty-nine hours been considered three days. It isn't even two full days of time (forty-eight hours), let alone the three days and three nights of death described in Jesus' self-prophecy in Matthew 12:40.

Realistic Biblical Interpretation

Chart 6

	Nisan 14 Jesus dies at 3PM	Nisan 15 High Sabbath	Nisan 16 Weekly Sabbath	Nisan 17 Jesus alive before sunrise
Day	1st Day Dead	2nd Day Dead	3rd Day Dead	**Alive**
	Nisan 15 High Sabbath	Nisan 16 Weekly Sabbath	**Nisan 17**	**Nisan 18**
Night	1st Night Dead	2nd Night Dead	3rd Night Dead	Appears to Disciples

In a more accurate review of the Bible scriptures, taking into account the High Priest of the Temple in charge of feast practices was of the ruling Sadducees sect, Jesus would die on Nisan 14th and rise on Nisan 17th, the Feast of First Fruits. This timeline would produce approximately sixty-three (63) hours of death, which is well beyond two days or forty-eight (48) hours. Sixty-three (63) hours would also qualify for Jesus literally rising on the third day.

3:00 PM Nisan 14th to 3:00 PM Nisan 15th = 24 hours

3:00 PM Nisan 15th to 3:00 PM Nisan 16th = 24 hours

3:00 PM Nisan 16th to 6:00 AM Nisan 17th = <u>15 hours</u>

Total   63 hours

    This biblical interpretation of the resurrection timeline would cover a period of three nights (Nisan 15th, Nisan 16th, Nisan 17th) and three days (daylight hours: Nisan 14th, Nisan 15th, Nisan 16th). The day portion of Nisan 17th would not qualify to be counted as "daylight" hours because Jesus rose from the grave before the sunrise. Thus, only the night hours could be counted for Nisan 17th.

    A Nisan 14th crucifixion with a Nisan 17th resurrection fulfills all Biblical prophecies regarding the time for death. It also fulfills the High Priest's sect requirement for Feast of First Fruits. Moreover, this time span is the only Biblical interpretation that correlates all New Testament scripture timelines without conflict or compromise of the Old and New Testament prophecies.

Chapter 10
Atonement: God's Design

Atonement has always been God's master plan for humanity. Long before Adam was created, before he brought sin to all mankind, and even before the very foundation of the world was laid, Jesus Christ was prepared to enter into flesh to redeem us (1 Peter 1:20). Throughout the Old Testament, God's master plan of redemption and atonement was hinted at in allegories, which pointed prophetically to Christ and occurred repeatedly on Nisan 17th. In the New Testament, God's plan of salvation was completed with the resurrection of Jesus on Nisan 17th.

This unique date in history has many themes associated with it in the Bible. The first occurred in the Old Testament when Noah's Ark rested on Mount Ararat. In Genesis salvation, deliverance from the wrath of God, and a new beginning for mankind combined on Nisan 17th. The symbolic meaning of the Ark landing on Mt. Ararat, which in Hebrew meant the "curse reversed" on Nisan 17th was also prophetic of the future date chosen by God when Jesus would reverse Adam's curse upon mankind. While no one should ever underestimate the power of Christ on the cross defeating sin, it was Jesus' resurrection that declared irrefutably the curse of sin and death was broken. The previous curse of death upon the children of Adam no longer reigned supreme. For those in Christ Jesus, death is swallowed up in victory (Isaiah 25:8, 1 Corinthians 15:54). Hence, the first mention of Nisan 17th in Genesis painted a vivid illustration of Jesus reversing Adam's curse on another mountain top by his death and with his future resurrection from the grave. Nisan 17th is a day signaling the redemption and new beginning for mankind.

Moving out of Genesis and into Exodus, a series of miraculous plagues led to the nation of Israel being released from slavery in Egypt. The final plague shook Pharaoh to his very core with the death of his first-born son. In despair, Pharaoh released Israel at first. Later as anger filled his heart, he determined to annihilate the nation and sent his army to chase them down.

It was along the shores of the Red Sea, God's children were trapped by certain death. The thunderous sound of horses' hooves and heavy chariots carried thousands of armed soldiers, making the dust rise into the sky like a large cloud. Israel knew death was imminent. Powerless to defend themselves against an enemy so formidable, they had no route of escape. There was no way to move forward. In fear and emotional agony, Israel called out to God for salvation.

The imagery in the Exodus story is spiritually symbolic of the condition of mankind without God's intervention. Humanity was trapped, defenseless, with no escape route left. Death was chasing after us. Then when all seemed lost, God suddenly moved onto the scene and placed Himself between the army of death and His children. God miraculously prepared a way by dividing the water, allowing passage on dry land through the sea. The impossible became possible with the intervention of God. His children were delivered from death by His mighty hand.

Moreover by God's power, Pharaoh's soldiers were drowned in the overflowing waters only after the Israelites safely crossed over. The drowning army before sunrise on Nisan 17th is a beautiful portrait of Jesus' resurrection. He forever swallowed up death in victory with the rising sun (1 Corinthians 15:54). Paul's metaphoric wording of "swallowing death" used in Corinthians brings to remembrance the watery image of the Red Sea swallowing up Pharaoh's army. Thus, the parallel of victory over death on Nisan 17th between the Old and New Testaments blend seamlessly.

All those who seek refuge in Christ are free from the fear of death pursuing them (Hebrews 2:15). The victory Christ gave to Believers was symbolized by Israel's excitement and celebration on the shores overlooking the Red Sea. They praise God at the sight of Egypt's power over them forever spoiled. Death was utterly destroyed. Standing on the shores of a new land, Israel for the first time in 400 years experiences true freedom from slavery.

Similarly, Believers in Jesus are delivered from slavery to sin, never to return to bondage of the enemy (Hebrews 2:15 and Romans 8:15). The power of Satan's army has been eliminated by the resurrection of the Son of God from the dead. Dawn brings a new life, a new beginning in a land filled with freedom. Like the Israelites dancing and praising along the shore, Believers rejoice with joy unspeakable (1Peter 1:8) at the wonder of God who has delivered them from death.

The Book of Joshua adds another dimension in the blessings of atonement to the prophecies associated with the date Nisan 17th. The story opens with Israel still in the wilderness, living literally day-to-day by a ration of the bread of Heaven. Manna while being a type of heavenly bread was not the real Bread of Heaven. Instead manna symbolized the Mosaic Law. In the Law, the blessings of God were given to mankind in increments based upon obedience. The Law provided blessings only so long as there remained total obedience to the Law or a sacrifice was offered for sin. The blessings of God were not continuous under the Law.

After surviving on manna forty long years in the wilderness, Israel finally entered into the Promised Land, flowing with milk and honey. Unfortunately, upon entering the Land of Promise, Israel was not immediately able to eat of its new grains. They had to wait until after the Feast of First Fruits sheaf offering had been waved before the Lord. Thankfully, manna was provided for them up until Nisan 16th, the day before the Feast of First Fruits. On the morning of Nisan 17th, as the High Priest waved the sheaf offering before the Lord, no manna fell. Instead, the people were free to eat of the land at will. For the first time since the leaving of Egypt, Israel ate fresh barley and other fruits from the Land of Promise.

While manna had been sustenance, the Israelites grew weary of eating the same flavor and texture, day after day, year after year. Now the Promised Land overflowed with variety. Whereas manna had been given only once a day, now there were no restrictions on the timing or availability of nourishment. Fresh fruits, vegetables, and numerous grains were available at their fingertips any time, day or night. A banquet of plenty lay before Israel, overflowing with diversity. Oh, the joy Israel must have experienced on Nisan 17th as the previous barriers were removed, and the abundance of food flourished, allowing them to freely partake at will.

Similarly, the Gospel of Grace given by Jesus Christ provides eternal and unlimited blessings from the Father to all who will believe. Unlike manna, the True Bread from Heaven has descended (John 6:32-33) to us, bringing life and nourishment to our souls. No longer is there a legalistic requirement to earn God's blessings (Romans 3:21-22), which were once rationed out based on obedience. Instead, by the sacrifice of Jesus. transference of His righteousness has been given to those who believe (Romans 5:19; 2 Corinthians 5:21). Believers partake of the continued blessings of Christ, becoming joint-heirs with Him (Romans 8:17). All spiritual blessings are theirs (Ephesians 1:3).

The fullness of the blessings of the Promised Land for Israel occurred on Nisan 17th when they were finally able to partake of the fruit of the land. The ability to enter into the blessings of the New Covenant of God, which began on the cross on Nisan 14th, culminated with the resurrection of Jesus on Nisan 17th. As a result of Jesus' resurrection, the New Covenant is confirmed. Humanity can now freely and continually eat from the spiritual Bread of Heaven, and every blessing in Christ is theirs.

Jesus is also a type of first fruits, being the first person raised by the Holy Spirit in eternal bodily form (1 Corinthians 15:2). Believers who have trusted in Christ will be raised at His return (1 Corinthians 15:23). They are the first fruits in the restorative creation process (James 1:18). Time will demonstrate God's ultimate plan before the foundation of the world was to elevate mankind from their previous position as mortal sons of God, to their true destiny as joint-heirs with Christ Jesus.

Yet, before this divine relationship and glory could be given to humanity, a sense of holy worship must be established in truth. Second Chronicles brings the revelation of true worship being restored to mankind on Nisan 17th, a necessity allowing direct access to God. After years of spiritual desolation and poverty, Israel's evil king was finally dead. A new king, a righteous king arises. The new king brought restitution to God's holy temple and assured sanctification of the priests. The time of cleansing and restoration was perfected on the morning of Nisan 17th, when King Hezekiah arose before dawn to gather the leaders and priests of Israel to the Temple and made sacrifices for the nation.

Correspondingly, the time of the reign of sin and evil that plagued the world is over. Selfish rulers driven by Satan appointed themselves in the land, controlling it through force and misery. However, spiritual restoration was brought back to mankind when a new ruler of the Earth assumed power. King Jesus, resurrected from the dead, had the temple of His body restored on the morning of Nisan 17th. His new body now cleansed from the sin of the world, which He carried on the cross. The impurities and sin of mortal flesh are forever removed. In their place stands a perfect, holy, and eternal temple.

This temple cleansed by the power of the Holy Spirit has been given to humanity (Romans 8:11). Through the giving of the Holy Spirit after Jesus' ascension to Heaven (John 16:7), for the first time in history, mankind has direct access to the throne of God (Hebrews 4:16). Through the Holy Spirit true worship has been restored to the original temple of God. Jesus prophetically announced the day when true worship would be restored beginning in John 4:23. He told the Samaritan woman at the well, "the time is coming and now is when the true worshippers shall worship the Father in spirit and in truth: for the Father seeks such to worship him."

Jesus was the first true worshipper, making a way to restore true worship for humanity the day He rose from the grave on Nisan 17th. Now Believers become living temples of God, being indwelt by the Holy Spirit (1 Corinthians 3:16). The gift of salvation, eternal blessings, and true worship are all part of the atonement of Christ. However, these aspects have not yet been revealed in their fullness for the world to see in bodily form.

This future revelation of the fullness of salvation's inheritance is the portrait of Nisan 17th outlined in the Book of Esther. Technically, the salvation of the nation of Israel began on Nisan 17th when King Ahasuerus gave the Jews' enemies to Queen Esther. On that day, the king killed Ha'man, transferred power to Mordecai, and wrote the decree of victory for the Jewish nation. Yet, it was not the final day of triumph, as there remained in Persia those who wanted to kill the Israelites. On Adar 13th, the children of Israel finally saw the fulfillment of their physical release from the previous death degree when the king's army rose up to defend them and slay their enemies. This allegory prophetically symbolized the ministry of Jesus, who upon His first coming freed Believers from the power of death. At Jesus' second coming, Believers will ultimately experience the redemption of their bodies. The new, eternal body will be the fullness of the triumph over death announced by Christ's resurrection on Nisan 17th.

Because of His finished work on the cross and resurrection from the grave, all the promises in Christ are "yes and amen," (2 Corinthians 1:20). Believers in Christ are indwelt by the Holy Spirit. They are holy temples of the Living God. However, there remains an interlude in time for Believers between Jesus' resurrection and the day their physical bodies are finally redeemed from decay and death at His second coming.

The ministry of Jesus Christ was to create redemption, sanctification, and salvation for humanity and destroy the works of the enemy. Nisan 17th is the date expressed throughout the Old Testament bringing life, hope, freedom, a new inheritance, true worship, and deliverance from death to the children of God. In the New Testament, all of these parable prophecies culminate with the resurrection of Jesus Christ from the dead on the morning of Nisan 17th.

God's original design for mankind has always been atonement. This is why God gave His only begotten Son to the world. Jesus made restitution for all those who will trust in God for their salvation. While there have been several thousand years between the fall of Adam and the redemption of His children back from sin, God has faithfully pursued us with love. His love knows no limits, and in the greatest display of love, God laid down His life for humanity. How incredible are works of God on Nisan 17th!

"$_{38}$For I am persuaded, that neither death, nor life, nor angels, nor principalities, nor powers, nor things present, nor things to come, $_{39}$Nor height, nor depth, nor any other creature, shall be able to separate us

from the love of God, which is in Christ Jesus our Lord."
Romans 8:38-89

Redemption's Secret: Understanding the Mystery of Nisan 17

BIBLIOGRAPHY

CHAPTER 3

1. Aubrey, Sharon *Jesus Unveiled*. Sutton, AK: Relevant Publishers LLC, 2015, pg 93.

CHAPTER 4

2. Aubrey, Sharon *Jesus Unveiled*. Sutton, AK: Relevant Publishers LLC, 2015, pg 99.

CHAPTER 8

3. Anatolius. ***The Paschal Canon of Anatolius of Alexandria.*** Section 11, 270- 280 AD. **Public Domain.**

4. Josephus, **Antiquities of the Jews** book 20, chapter 9, section 1. **Public Domain.**

INDEX
OF ILLUSTRATIONS & CHARTS

	DESCRIPTION	PAGE #
Illustration 1	Hebrew Day	9
Chart 1	Comparison of Jewish/Roman/ Gregorian Hours	10
Chart 2	Hebrew Days of the Week	10
Chart 3	Jewish Order of Months	15
Chart 4	Days of Manna	50
Chart 5	Traditional Church Teaching	66
Chart 6	Realistic Biblical Interpretation	68

Are you interested in hosting a Bible study
or discussion group on
the topics discussed in this book?

Check out our **FREE** resources
available online at

www.relevantpublishers.com

Want a deeper understanding of events
in the Crucifixion Week?

Check out

Jesus Unveiled
by Sharon Aubrey

www.ingramcontent.com/pod-product-compliance
Lightning Source LLC
Chambersburg PA
CBHW050443010526
44118CB00013B/1662